Preschool - Kinde

Cut and Paste
PUZZLES

Help your child develop:

- ✓ Scissor skills
- ✓ Logical reasoning
- ✓ Critical thinking
- ✓ Fine motor skills
- ✓ Hand-eye coordination

Dear Parents and Caregivers,

These puzzles will help your child develop their scissor skills as well as problem solving, patience, hand-eye coordination and more. Help your children cut out the images. Put the puzzle together and paste it onto a paper.

Have fun together!
Teacher Veronica ☺

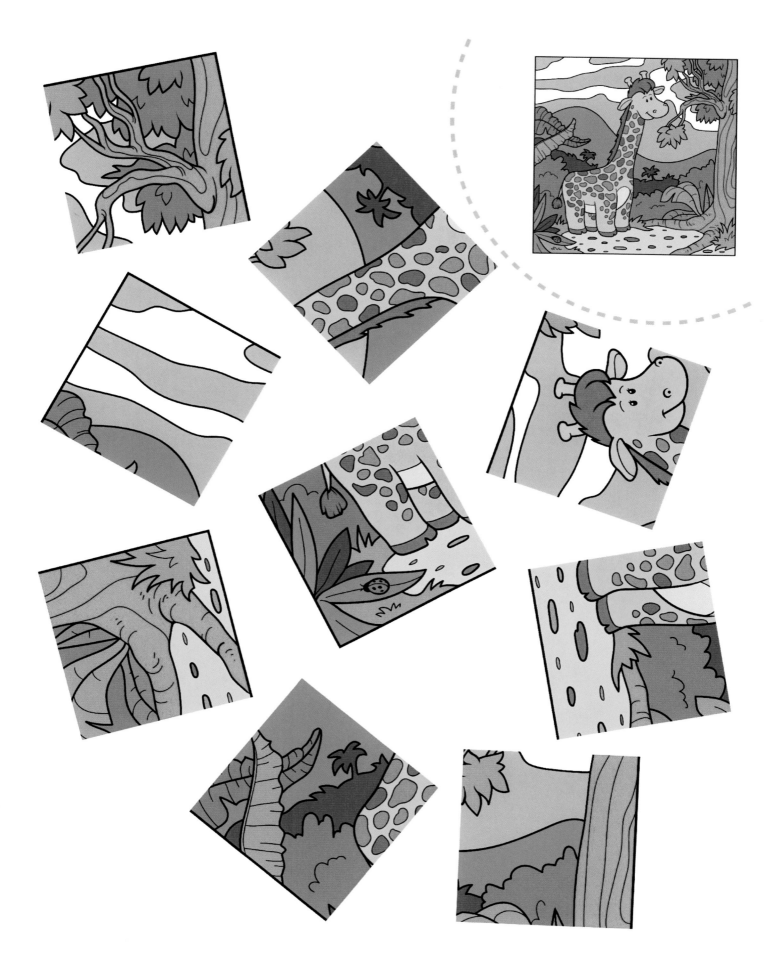

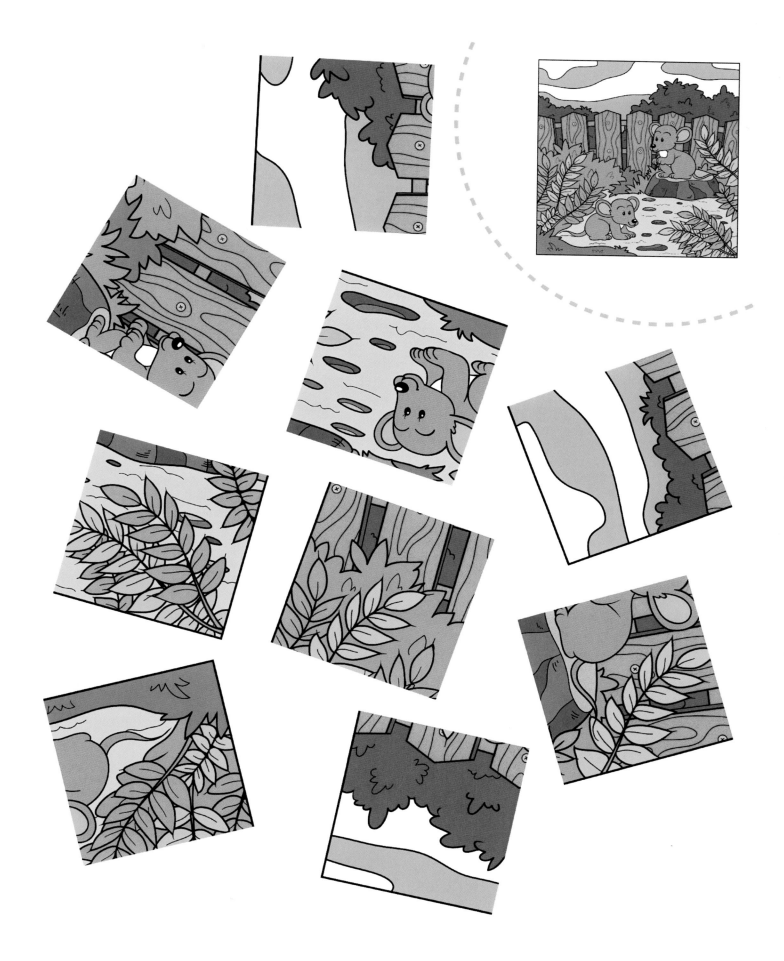

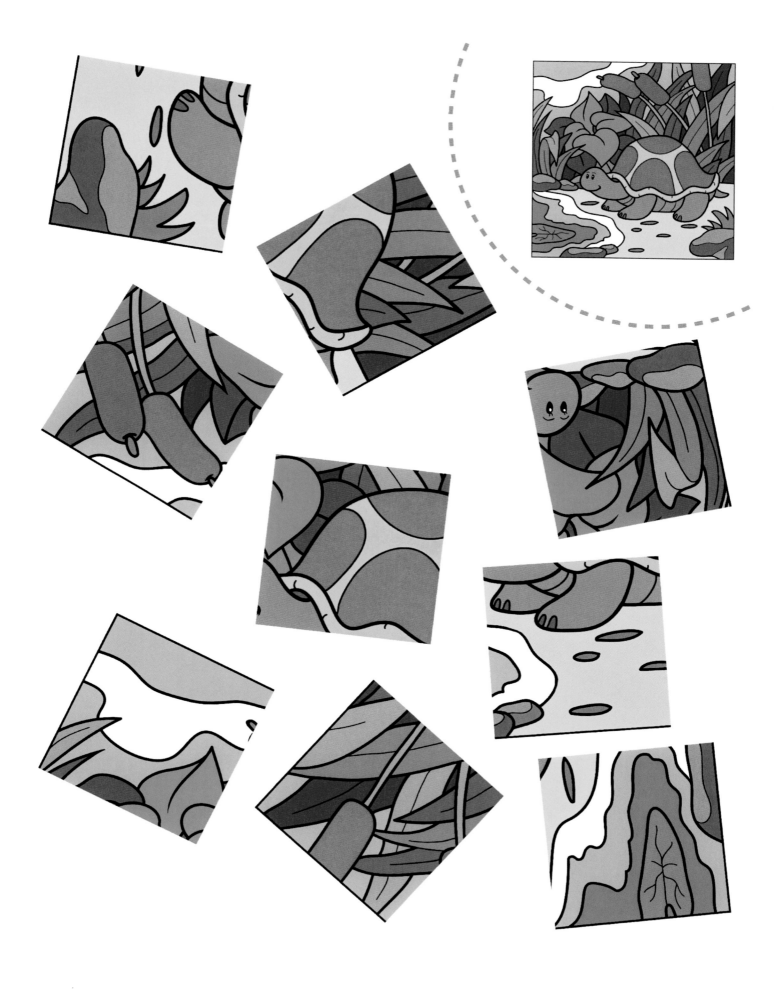

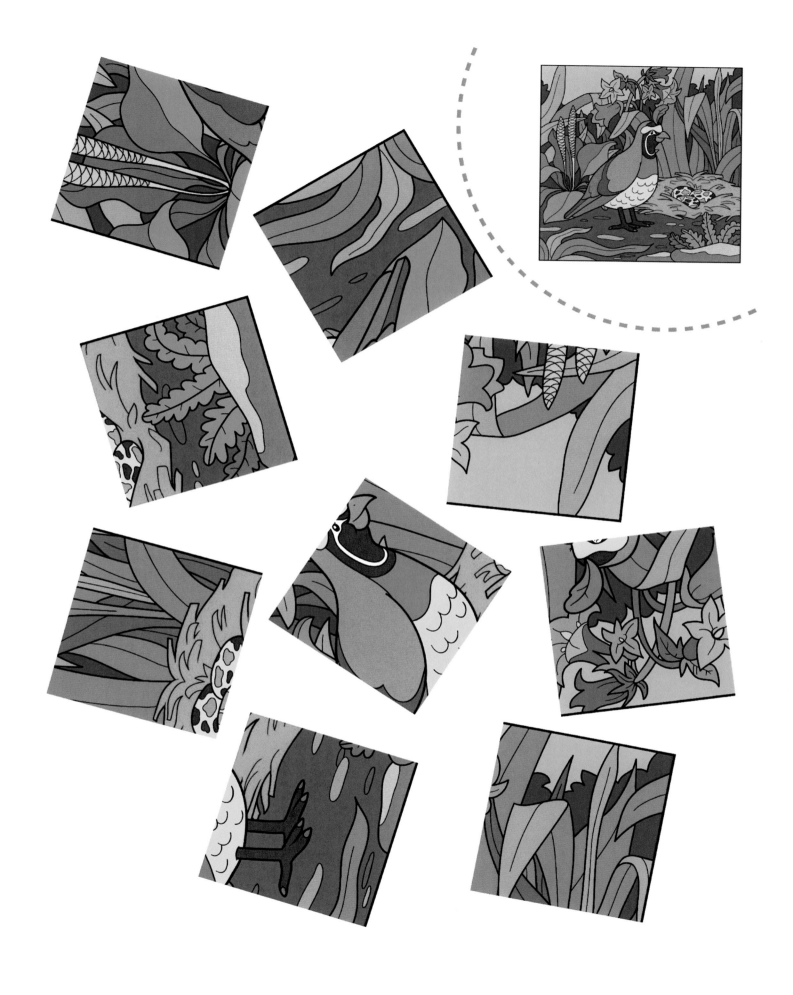

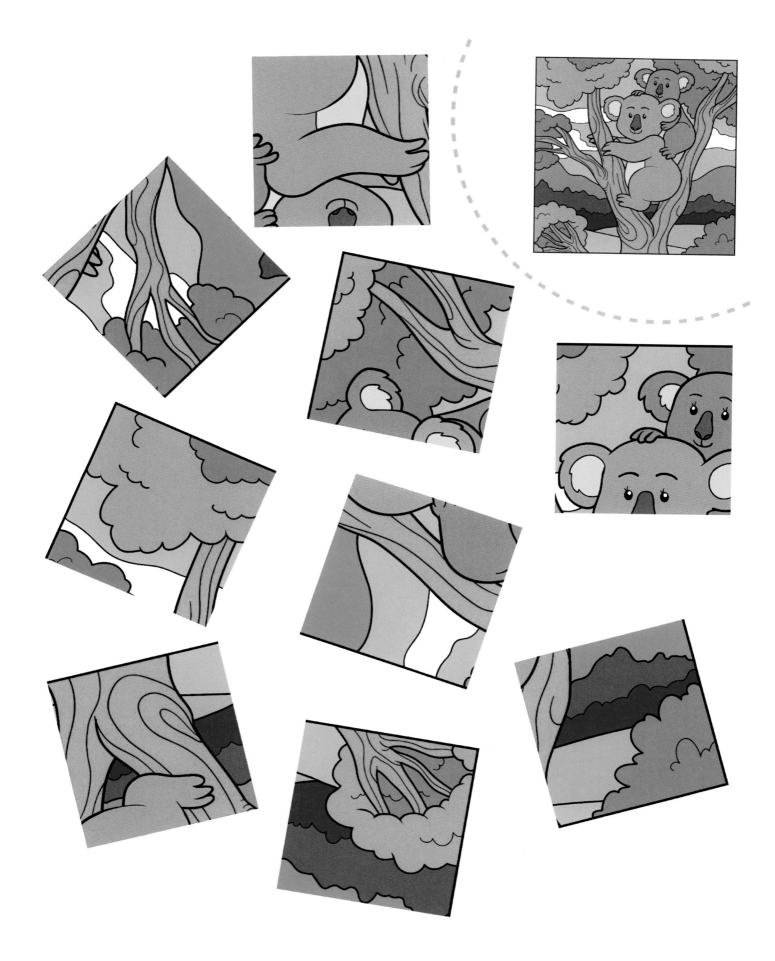

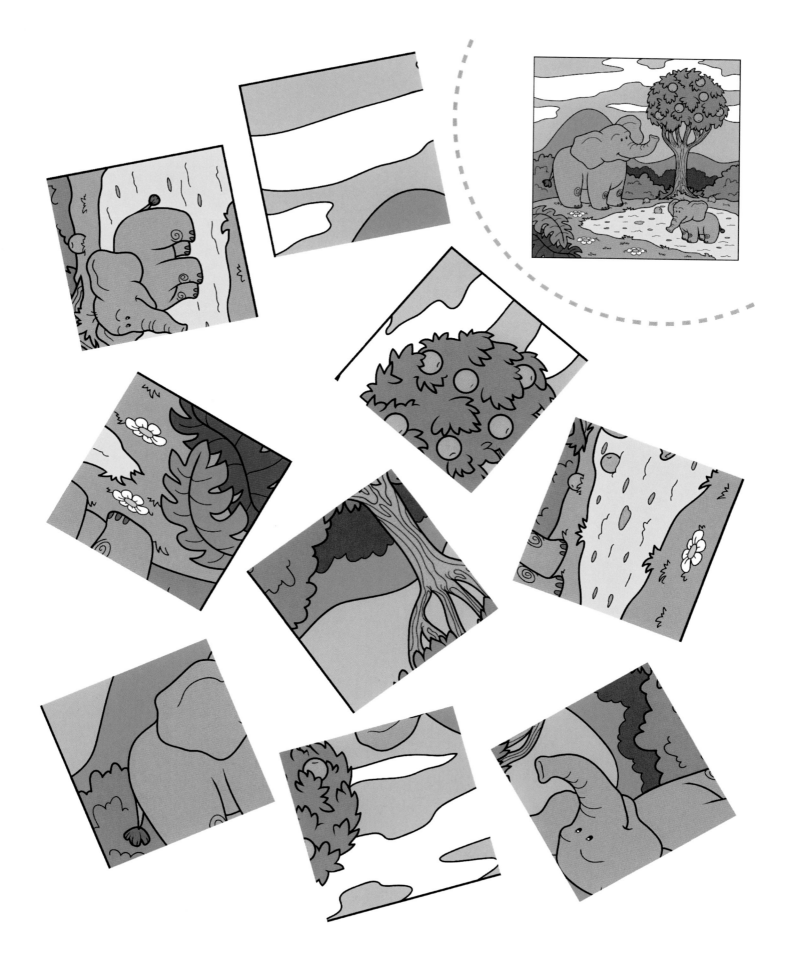

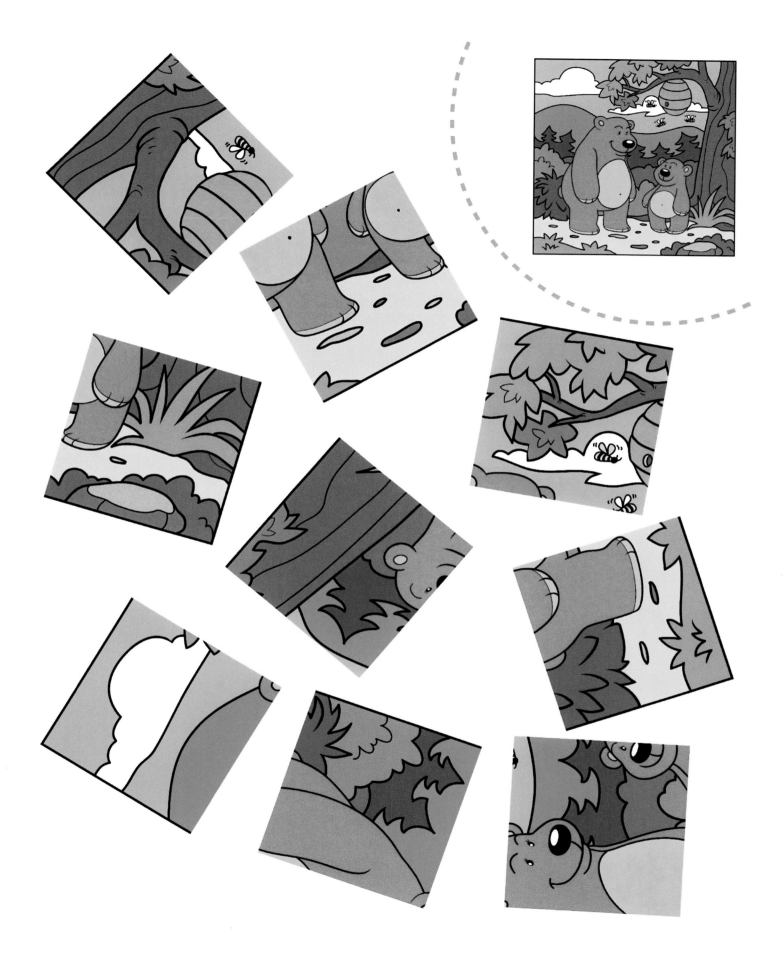

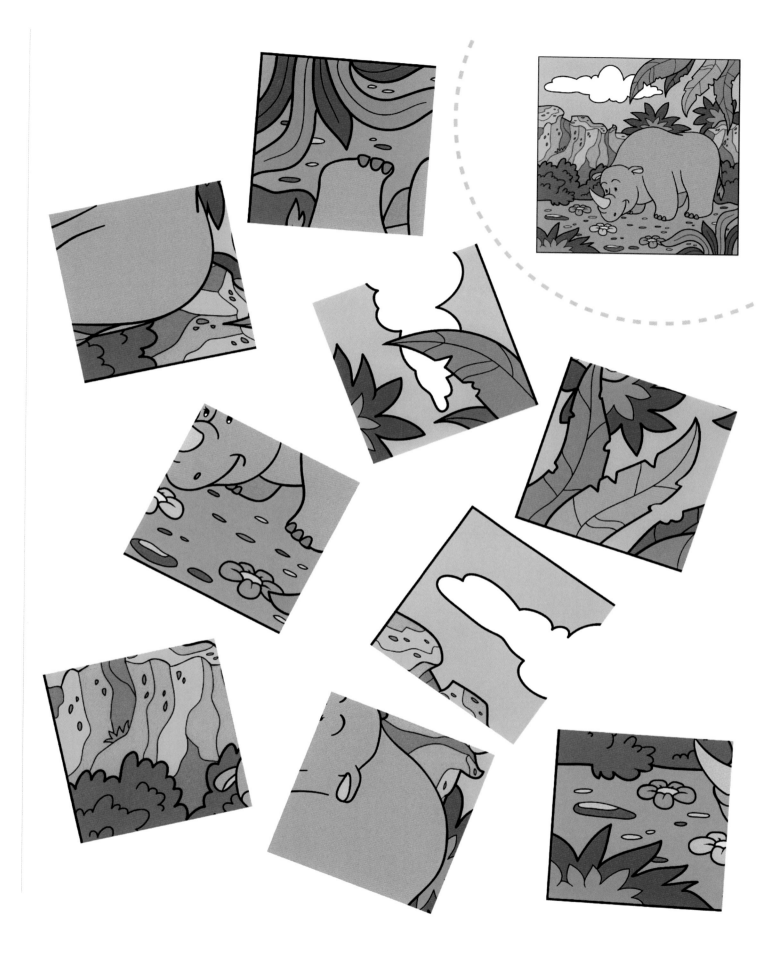

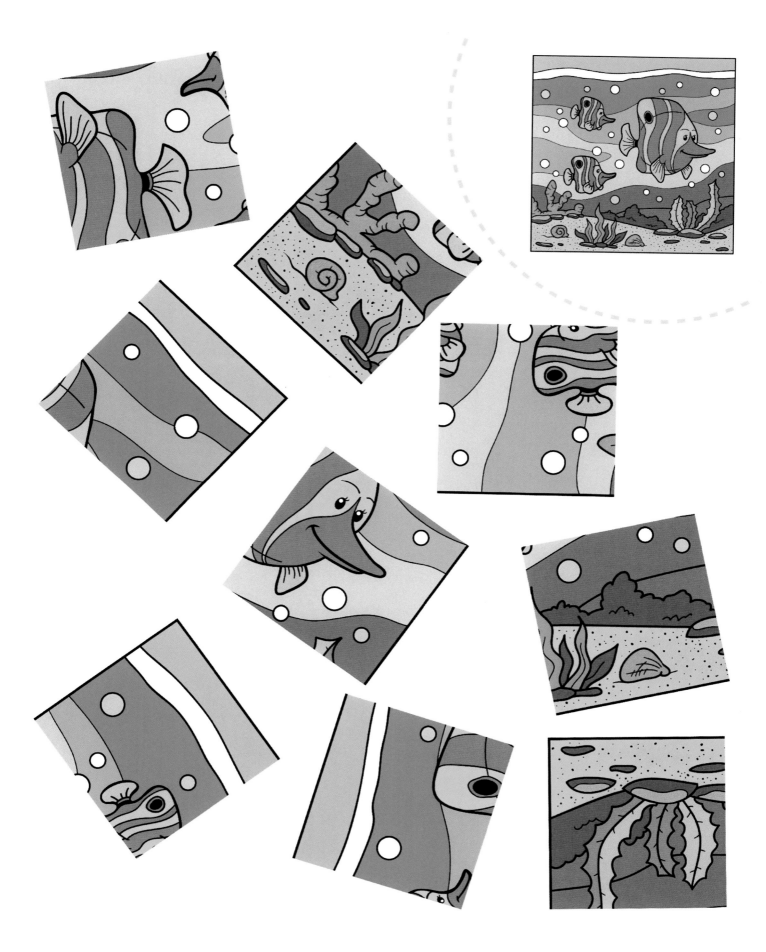

Made in the USA
Monee, IL
06 September 2020